DO YOU KNOW

Dinosaurs?

Written by
Alain M. Bergeron
Michel Quintin
Sampar

Illustrations by
Sampar

Translated by
Solange Messier

Fitzhenry & Whiteside

First published as "Savais-Tu? Les Dinosaures" by Editions Michel Quintin, Québec, Canada

Published in Canada by Fitzhenry & Whiteside, 195 Allstate Parkway, Markham, Ontario L3R 4T8

Published in the United States by Fitzhenry & Whiteside, 311 Washington Street, Brighton, Massachusetts 02135

www.fitzhenry.ca   godwit@fitzhenry.ca

10 9 8 7 6 5 4 3 2 1

Library and Archives Canada Cataloguing in Publication
Do You Know Dinosaurs?
ISBN 9781554553365 (pbk.)
Data available on file

Publisher Cataloging-in-Publication Data (U.S.)
Do You Know Dinosaurs?
ISBN 9781554553365 (pbk.)
Data available on file

Fitzhenry & Whiteside acknowledges with thanks the Canada Council for the Arts, and the Ontario Arts Council for their support of our publishing program. We acknowledge the financial support of the Government of Canada through the Canada Book Fund (CBF) for our publishing activities.

Cover and text design by Daniel Choi
Cover image by Sampar
Printed in China by Sheck Wah Tong Printing Press Ltd.

During the **Age of Dinosaurs,** humans didn't exist yet. In fact, humans appeared 65 million years after the last dinosaur disappeared.

Dinosaurs appeared approximately 250 million years ago. They reigned on earth for 160 million years.

Gigantic insects also lived during the Age of Dinosaurs. Dragonflies were 75 centimetres (29 inches) long and cockroaches were 30 centimetres (12 inches) long.

Dinosaurs are **reptiles**. The term "dinosaur" means "terrible lizard." All dinosaurs lived on land, even if they did go in the water occasionally.

Mammals, fish, **amphibians**, and other reptiles, such as the flying Pteranodons and the marine Plesiosaurs, also lived during this period.

To this day, approximately 800 dinosaur **species**, of all shapes and sizes, have been identified.

While some dinosaurs were huge, others were tiny. The Compsognathus was without a doubt the smallest of them all. It was barely the size of a chicken.

The Ultrasaurus is the largest dinosaur ever discovered. It could reach 18 metres (59 feet) in height, which is as tall as a 5-storey building.

The Ultrasaurus also holds the record as the heaviest dinosaur. It could attain a weight of 135,000 kilograms (297,600 pounds)—the size of 25 large African elephants.

The Brachiosaurus is one of the tallest known dinosaurs. It weighed more than 80,000 kilograms (176,400 pounds) and could reach a length of 24 metres (79 feet) and a height of 12 metres (39 feet).

The Brachiosaurus could eat an equivalent of 35 bales of hay every day.

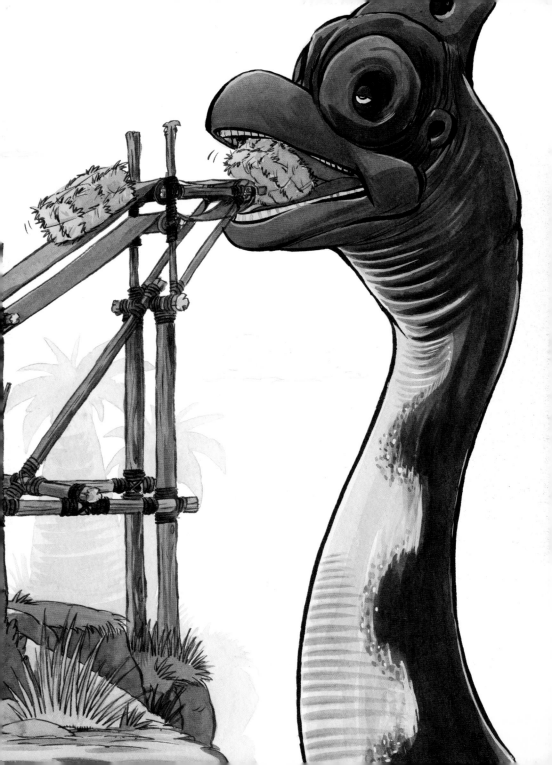

The Diplodocus is one of the longest dinosaurs on record. This longneck measured approximately 30 metres (98 feet) from its head to the tip of its tail, which is equivalent to the length of 3 school buses.

The Apatosaurus was as heavy as 6 large elephants. Its footprint could contain up to 80 litres (21 gallons) of water, which could fill a swimming pool.

The majority of dinosaurs were peaceful **herbivores.** Scientists believe that several species ate 100 kilograms (220 pounds) of leaves per day.

Other dinosaurs were **carnivores**. The Tyrannosaurus rex was the largest of the meat-eaters. It was as tall as 3 people stacked on top of each other.

The Tyrannosaurus rex, with its long, sharp teeth the size of human hands, could rip apart flesh in strips. It is likely the most terrifying **predator** of any time period.

Some herbivorous dinosaurs were covered in bony armour that made them almost invulnerable. The Ankylosaurus was completely covered by this armour.

Some dinosaurs were also equipped with deadly weapons. The Triceratops defended itself with its 3 horns.

The Stegosaurus defended itself by swinging its tail around like a club. Its tail proved to be a dangerous weapon against its opponents, especially because it was armed with long spikes.

Regardless of the fact that it was 6 metres (20 feet) long and weighed 2,000 kilograms (4,400 pounds), the Stegosaurus holds the record for having the tiniest brain in relation to size.

At only 85 grams (0.03 ounces), its brain wasn't any bigger than a walnut.

While some dinosaurs were unbalanced and moved slowly, others could run quickly—perhaps even as fast as horses.

The fastest was the Ornithomimus, an ostrich-like dinosaur.

Dinosaurs built nests and laid eggs. The largest egg on record was the size of a football.

Even though most dinosaurs had teeth, some did not. The Oviraptor, for example, had only a beak, which resembled that of a parrot's.

The Anatosaurus, a duck-billed dinosaur, had a record set of 2,000 teeth.

53

Some dinosaurs, like the Oviraptor, fed on the eggs of other dinosaurs.

Everyone brings what they can contribute to the meal, my friend.

Some dinosaurs had really hard heads. The Pachycephalosaurus's skull bone was 25 centimetres (10 inches) thick. Its skull, similar to a helmet, protected its brain during battle.

No one really knows why dinosaurs disappeared. They may have died out because of **famine**, disease, cold weather, or several other reasons.

Glossary

Age of Dinosaurs the Mesozoic Era, which is separated into the Triassic, Jurassic and Cretaceous periods

Amphibian a cold-blooded, back-boned animal, such as a frog, newt or salamander

Carnivore a meat-eater

Famine a period of mass starvation when food is hard to find

Herbivore an animal that eats only plants

Mammal a warm-blooded, back-boned animal

Predator a hunter that kills prey for food

Reptile a cold-blooded, back-boned animal covered in scales or hard parts, such as a snake, lizard or crocodilian

Species a classification for a group of creatures with common characteristics

Index

Do You Know there are other titles?

Rats

Crows

Porcupines

Crocodiles

Toads

Chameleons

Spiders

Leeches

Hyenas

Komodo Dragons

Praying Mantises